AMAZING AUSTRALIA

A Traveler's Guide to Common Plants and Animals

LAINE CUNNINGHAM

AMAZING AUSTRALIA
A Traveler's Guide to Common Plants and Animals

Copyright © 2018 Laine Cunningham

Published by Sun Dogs Creations
Changing the World One Book at a Time

Cover Design by Angel Leya

ISBN: 9781946732774

All rights reserved. No part of this book may be reproduced in any form or by any means, electronic, mechanical, digital, photocopying or recording, except for the inclusion in a review, without permission in writing from the publisher. Thank you for supporting authors and a diverse, creative culture by purchasing this book and complying with copyright laws.

Table of Contents

Introduction 1

FLORA 5

FAUNA 15

   MAMMALS 16

      MARSUPIALS 16

      MONOTREMES 23

      OTHER MAMMALS 25

   INSECTS AND ARACHNIDS 27

   REPTILES 32

   AMPHIBIANS 36

   MARINE LIFE 37

   BIRDS 45

The Dance: An Australian Aboriginal Dreamtime Guide to Living with Passion, Adapted from *Seven Sisters: Spiritual Messages from Aboriginal Australia* 53

Also by Laine Cunningham 58

Introduction

How very many things I used to be.

Recently I began looking toward the milestone of turning fifty years old. It would be poetic, I suppose, to claim that at milestones like birthdays and New Year's I pause to take stock of what my life has been and what it might yet become...a pretty claim, yet one that would be false.

Instead, reflection is more frequently an ongoing process, one that arises in small glimpses snatched while we are busy at some chore that leads our minds idle in the midst of activity — doing the dishes, perhaps, or weeding the garden. Travel, of course, is one of those things, particularly when you leave your job, sell off everything you own, and fly halfway around the world to spend six months camping along in the rugged Australian Outback.

Some years ago I did just that. On nights spent in blessedly expansive solitude, I learned to play the didgeridoo. Every evening I cooked over an open fire and then huddled next to the embers for warmth while watching the Milky Way grow brighter. On the roads and in the bush, I saw animals and plants and birds that most travelers do not...unless they visit a zoo, where they find bored captives living in tiny cages.

I fled that same type of cage, of corporate boredom and stultifying sameness, for the experiences I would discover in the desert. *Woman Alone,* the memoir of that journey, touches on some of the ways those months changed me. And so even today I arise in the depths of night, after my body has rested and my mind has quieted the day's chatter, to review some of the many things I no longer am.

The course of our years is blessedly long. During these decades, we live many lives as daughters and sisters, lovers and wives. We become parents than launch our children into the world or lose them to the next; we teach another's child the wisdom we would give our own; we learn those lessons our parents were not equipped to provide.

Each of these steps makes us something different. We gain some things deliberately or accidentally; we shed others or use them in a process that only time or a different changeling can experience as something other than grief. Travel—even the most luxurious kind, even that which keeps us imprisoned on a bus for hours or allows us only minutes in a transcendent state—has the same impact. It makes us anew.

With each new person we become, we experience rebirth. Each rebirth is of necessity a death, a closing of some part of who we were that allows us to become. There is chaos and pain but if we release our expectations of the lives we have led up until that moment, we can discover joy. It hurts to leave behind the friends and things that no longer serve who we become; this pain is grief, and that grief honors the very special places people had held in our lives. When we finally part, we turn to the new self and begin a new life.

If we could see back into the lives of those left behind, we might discover that they too have been reborn, that our place in their lives was similarly complete. Travel allows us to do this, too, in a way. It shows us new people and places, and allows us to find the shining pieces of ourselves in these new places...like greeting old friends we have just now met.

My brother and I grew up on the move. Every two or three years found my family in a new city or town, transplanted to a new state or country where lives and expectations were very different from the ones before. In addition to the opportunities each move gave us to expand our awareness of the world, it also forced us into rebirth.

Over and over we were given the chance to become something different. It wasn't entirely a free choice, as our status as new arrivals to schools where many of the other kids had known each other for years made us outsiders who were often unwelcome. Yet our status as unknowns allowed us to present whatever we felt we were at that time.

This wasn't a conscious process, but one that I later recognized. People who live together for years take certain things for granted. They lock their friends and neighbors into a set of expectations based on what they used to be.

We see this dynamic during every holiday when families impose their creaky dynamics on adult children and siblings treat people as who they were rather than what they are. Only the dearest friends can see that which we have become. Only they are dear enough to our hearts to share in our rebirth, and only they hold us dear enough to allow us to change.

How very many things I used to be.

How very many things I will become.

As you browse through this short guide to the most common animals and plants in Australia, I hope that you look forward to your own journey— its discoveries, its beauties, its challenges, and your own renewal.

LAINE CUNNINGHAM

FLORA

Acacia A.k.a. wattle. The acacia, one of the two most prevalent species in the country besides the eucalypt, appears on the Australian national coat of arms. Australian wattles account for nearly 3/4 of the world's acacias. Acacias as a group are quickly identified by the tendency of the bark to curl on the stem. All produce yellow or cream flowers and bean-shaped pods, belying their relation to pea plants. See entries for *ironwood, mulga,* and *witchetty.*

Banksia The banksias are named for the botanist who discovered them, Sir Joseph Banks. Of 71 species, all of which prefer sandy soil, 57 are found only in Western Australia. Hundreds of yellow flowers ranging in color from cream to reddish-brown cluster in 12-inch spikes or cones. In tree form, the banksia may grow up to 66 feet tall. As a shrub, the plant may attain 45 feet of height and will be more spread out.

Blood gum These eucalypts are named for the thick red sap that oozes from cracks in the bark or from injuries to the trunk or branches. These trees are identified by the flaky grey bark with salmon splotches. The fruit capsules, or gum nuts, are much larger than those of other eucalypts. Outer branches may sport "apples," burls caused by insects living inside. The insects were often eaten by Aboriginal tribes.

Coolabah The coolabah is the hardiest of all the eucalypt species, withstanding frost and temperatures in excess of 120° F. It grows to 80 feet in height, and its timber can weigh 80 pounds per cubic foot.

Corkwood Members of the wood family are distinguished by clusters of white or off-white flowers, each with a long stamen. The thick, deeply grooved bark protects the trees from fire. Flames intense enough to kill the long-leaf corkwood will cause the woody pods to release winged seeds that flutter away on the updrafts.

Epiphyte This category includes mosses, lichens, fungi, ferns, vines, flowering plants, and some orchids. All are characterized by a lack of woody stalk or supporting structure, and none will have roots in the soil. Epiphytes attach themselves to the trunks or branches of trees, and hang on with a system of clinging roots.

By living high in the canopy, they receive light without having to grow tall like plants rooted in soil. Water draining down the bark and rotting leaves, fruit, and debris piled up around the epiphyte's roots nourish the plant. Some, such as the bird's-nest fern, grow broad leaves that encircle the host's trunk to collect larger amounts of falling debris.

Eucalypt A.k.a. gum tree. Closely related species of eucalypts hybridize easily. Even though over 700 varieties have been classified, new species are still being found. Eucalypts appear in numerous forms, from the stunted mallee shaped by the harsh environment to the robust specimens towering over 300 feet high. The eucalypt is the world's most-transplanted tree. The fast-growing species are often used for windbreaks in agriculture.

The leaves, unlike those of other trees, are layered with photosynthetic cells on both sides. Dangling straight down, the leaves collect sunlight from both sides to take full advantage of this abundant resource. The fruits, or gum nuts, are actually flowers. The cap of each nut is fashioned from petals that have fused together to protect the stamens beneath. When the cap pops off, the stamens display their white, red, or pink glory to attract pollinating insects.

Ghost gum Named for the smooth white trunk that seems to glow in the dusk. The gum nuts of this tree are smooth and lack the four beaks of the *red river gum* (see). A powdery dust covering the bark is used by Aboriginal people for body decoration during ceremonies.

Ironwood With its drooping leaves, this tree's outline resembles a weeping willow. The pods are pinched between each seed, and the narrow leaves have parallel veins. The timber is exceptionally hard and durable, and was used by Aboriginal tribes to make tools and weapons.

Kangaroo paw Western Australia's official state flower, the kangaroo paw looks exactly like its name. About three feet tall, the red and green plant terminates in a group of curved, claw-like tips that are fuzzy and soft to the touch.

Mountain ash This is the largest eucalypt, second only to California's towering sequoias. The trunks may be 300 feet high and 10 feet in diameter.

Mulga This acacia is the most common tree in central Australia, and has lent its name to the phrase "go mulga," meaning to travel into the bush. The leaf shapes may be anywhere from flat and wide to rounded and narrow, so identification is best made by the upward-pointing leaves and branches. This hardwood was used by Aboriginal people to make durable tools and weapons such as spears, digging sticks, and shields.

Native fig This shrub may occur as a tree, but both forms will have broad, shiny leaves and fruit at the point where the leaves attach to the branches.

In exchange for a place to lay her eggs, a tiny wasp will enter the fruit through a pinhole and pollinate the flowers inside. The flowers never see sunlight, developing entirely within the capsule, and the wasp herself never emerges again. Gaining entrance to the fruit usually tears off her wings and antennae, and she will die inside. This symbiotic relationship is thought to be over a million years old.

Orchid Of the various orchids native to Australia, at least a few have developed in ways as unusual as the animals. The *Galeola foliata* of northern New South Wales and Queensland climbs rainforest trees and can be almost 50 feet long. Two other orchids spend their lives underground, the only ones in the world to do so.

River red gum The river red gum is the most widely distributed of all eucalypts in mainland Australia, and is highly adaptable to arid conditions. True to its name, the red-timbered tree prefers low-lying areas where rainwater will collect, the flood plains of creeks and rivers, and the seasonal watercourses of arid regions.

These trees put down two root systems. One is deep to tap underground water supplies, while the other is wide and shallow to soak up the occasional rains. During drought, the tree will cut off the nutrient supply to certain branches and let them drop to the ground to conserve water.

Up to 125 feet tall, the river red gum is capable of growing new bark if damage occurs during bushfires. The best identifier of this tree is the gum nut, which has four prominent beaks protruding from the cap.

Snake vine This remainder from the days when the interior was covered with lush jungle occurs mainly in the Osborne Range between Barrow Creek and Wycliffe Well, NT. The dark green vine climbs trees and in winter sheds its leaves, an unusual habit for desert plants. Aboriginal people tied the pounded stems around their heads to cure headache, rubbed the sap on sores, and covered wounds with its leaves.

Spinifex The Greek term for one of the two genera of spinifex grass means "spear point," and the sharp points of the dried grass live up to that name. Explorer Ernest Giles cursed all 30 species of spinifex as "abominable vegetable," and for good reason. The grasses are classified as hard or soft depending on whether you can grab a handful without puncturing your hand.

AMAZING AUSTRALIA

Fresh blades of spinifex are green and relatively inoffensive. During the first dry spell, the blades fold shut and become hard. The fibrous leaves are embedded with silica granules. When the leaves fold over, the silica protrudes and slices the skin of anyone passing by.

The majority of Australia's inland vegetation is spinifex, which has been classified as the hardiest grass in the world. The plants form hummock grasslands, growing in circular clumps up to 20 feet across. The older, central portions die off as stems on the periphery regenerate. Livestock will not touch the grass, and even the kangaroos will avoid a mouthful of ground glass.

Spinifex is not entirely useless, however. Growth is slow during drought, but after a good rain, spinifex produces flowers. They provide nectar and food to various animals and birds. The Aboriginal people ground the seeds into flour and manufactured glue from spinifex resin. Although the process is extremely labor intensive, the resulting product is harder and more durable than some industrial plastics.

Staghorn fern This epiphyte gains its name from the shape of its leaves, with lobes that fork out in a shape reminiscent of deer horns. Seeds form on the underside of the leaves and may be visible from the ground only as a reddish-brown stain. When ready, the seeds will be released to the wind to land on another tree. Also see entry under *epiphyte* for general information.

Strangler fig The seeds of the native fig are deposited on other trees by birds and rainforest animals. The seed sends roots as thin as dental floss down the trunk. Aerial roots can be 90 feet long. Once the roots can draw nutrients from the soil, the crown begins to develop to reach sunlight. The strangler's roots grow thicker and stronger as the host tree continues to grow. Eventually the host will crush itself against the girdle of roots and will rot away, leaving the fig's roots to support the tree.

Stinging gympie This plant was named for the town where it was first discovered, and what a painful revelation it was. The stems and heart-shaped leaves of this tropical species are coated with tiny hairs. Each hollow hair is filled with poison, and contact with the plant causes a tingling sensation that becomes extremely painful within 20 seconds. The torment can last several days before abating, and can recur for as much as 18 months whenever the site becomes wet. The only treatment is to remove the hairs from the skin with sticky tape.

Sturt's Desert Pea These gorgeous vines sprout after a rain and begin blossoming in a few weeks. The vibrant red petals loop gracefully around the black base, and are a colorful addition to the desert's flora.

Sundew The sundew is a carnivorous plant, relying on meat to make up for the lack of nutrients in the poor soil. Sticky hairs lure insects near with their fragrance and color, and then trap the prey in a gooey nightmare. The hairs, which are actually organs, secrete digestive enzymes and absorb the liquid meal.

AMAZING AUSTRALIA

Tea tree A.k.a. melaleuca. This category includes over 120 species of small trees. The fragrant oil is still used today as an antiseptic and for mild rashes and other skin conditions.

Upside-down plant This plant sports leafless stems to prevent vapor loss. The plant received its unusual name because it produces large red pea flowers at the base. The position protects the delicate blossoms from the blistering sun and desiccating wind. The flowers' nectar is edible, and was eaten by Aboriginal people.

Wattle See entry under *acacia.*

Wild orange Australia supports three species of this tree, which were an important source of food for the Aboriginal tribes. The wild orange produces a yellow-green fruit with a taste that is initially pleasing, but which is followed by a kerosene aftertaste. The weeping wild orange is the most palatable, and the oval fruit splits open when ripe. A third variety occurs as a vine, but is uncommon.

Witchetty bush Another type of *acacia* (see), this shrub has smooth bark on its many stems and slightly wider leaves than the *mulga* (see). It may grow up to ten feet tall and is home to the larval *witchetty grub* (see entry under Insects and Arachnids).

LAINE CUNNINGHAM

FAUNA

MAMMALS

MARSUPIALS

Marsupials are mammals, the female of which has a marsupium, an external abdominal pouch, instead of a placenta. The mammary glands are located inside the marsupium and the pouch protects the young until they are fully developed. Marsupial species include the kangaroos and their cousins: wallabies, euros, bandicoots, and kangaroo rats. Possums are also marsupials, and are one of the few found outside Australia.

***

Bandicoot Like the pouch of other marsupials that walk on four legs, the bandicoot's pouch faces backward to keep out dirt. Bandicoots primarily feast on grubs and slugs. Their apparent lack of ferocity disappears when battling a rival. The bandicoot gashes its enemies with powerful blows from its hind claws.

Bilby This is a rabbit-eared subspecies of the *bandicoot* (see). The creature is highly adaptable, and survived invasive species by moving into more arid regions.

Brush-tailed rat kangaroo This marsupial is one of many that sports a prehensile tail. The rat kangaroo uses its tail to haul grass to its nest. The tail loops neatly around a bundle before the rat kangaroo hops away.

AMAZING AUSTRALIA

Honey possum Also see general information under the entry for *possum*. The tiny honey possum resides on the southwestern coast and prefers to eat nectar. The possum hangs by its prehensile tail to reach blossoms, and bristles on the end of its inch-long tongue soak up nectar and pollen. Insects trapped in the nectar provide protein.

Kangaroo Kangaroos run the gambit, growing up to 7 feet tall and 200 pounds, or as little as a few inches high and a few ounces. They may climb trees, live among rocky cliffs, or nest in swamps and live on plains. Jumps of 25 feet are routine, but when pressed the leaps can span 40 feet. Speeds can exceed 40 mph.

Kangaroos swim quite well. Paddling with their forepaws keeps their heads above water. Strong kicks from their hind legs propel them forward. The hide provides excellent leather, and the meat of its tail is lean and tasty.

Koala Although eucalypt leaves are toxic to most other creatures, the koala's elaborate digestive system and special enzymes turn the leaves into a palatable meal. The koala's sense of smell is highly developed, and it will sniff the leaves before choosing which ones to eat. It might be testing the leaf's chemical content, as it never eats young eucalypt leaves. This specialized diet provides almost everything the koala desires. The animal will occasionally eat soil for calcium and minerals, but extracts all the water it needs from gum leaves.

The only arboreal marsupial without a visible tail, the koala has strong claws and opposable thumbs on its forepaws. The creature spends as much as 18 hours a day sleeping in the fork of a tree, saving what little energy it gains from its poor diet. A fleshy pad on the rear end provides adequate cushioning for long slumbers. Koalas are mostly nocturnal, and can live up to twelve years in the wild.

These tree-dwelling animals are slow except during mating time, when they chase away other males or pursue unwilling females. Mating occurs in the early spring and midsummer, and the female will produce one cub every other year after a gestation of 35 days. The young emerge from the pouch at about six months of age, and continue to use the pouch for about two months. From then until one year of age, the young travel piggyback by clinging to the mother.

Numbat A.k.a. banded anteater. This seven-inch marsupial's diet consists mainly of termites. The numbat's head tapers into a muzzle that harbors a four-inch-long sticky tongue. The forepaws are equipped with heavy claws for digging into mounds. The body is banded with rust stripes on white fur, lending it the English name.

Possum Of the various types of possums found in Australia, the brush-tailed is seen most often. Highly adaptable, the brush-tailed prefers forested areas and reproduces once or twice a year after a gestation of only 17 days.

AMAZING AUSTRALIA

The mountain brush-tailed and northern brush-tailed possums sport different coloration, but all are nocturnal and live in trees. Their diet consists of leaves, tender shoots, fruit, flowers, seeds, bark, insects, and other small animals. Possums mark and defend their territory with scent signals, and often rub the scent glands on their chests onto tree trunks and branches.

Quokka A.k.a. short-tailed wallaby or short-tailed pademelon. Found in coastal southwestern Australia, these endangered creatures are concentrated on Rottnest Island. The female mates while the first offspring is developing in the pouch. If the first offspring dies within six months, the second will develop and be born. This behavior, common among marsupials, increases the female's chance of bearing at least one young per season.

Tasmanian devil As little as 600 years ago, the devil inhabited the mainland, but it might have been killed off by dingoes. Found only in Tasmania, the devil is the largest of the carnivorous marsupials. Surprisingly noisy for a predator, the devil will scream when angered.

By day the devil rests in hollow logs, rock crevices or caves. It emerges at dusk to feed on small creatures and carrion. A slow and clumsy runner, the devil ambushes prey and uses its powerful jaws to kill and to crack the bones it eats. Roughly the size of a Cocker Spaniel, the Tasmanian devil has powerful forequarters and massive teeth.

Tasmanian pademelon A.k.a. rufous wallaby or red-bellied pademelon. This marsupial hides by day in dense scrub, forming tunnel-like runways through thick underbrush. At night it emerges to feed on grasses, herbs, and woody plants. When alarmed, it signals others with a thump of its foot.

Tasmanian tiger A.k.a. thylacine or Tasmanian wolf. This marsupial wolf was built like a German Shepherd, and was roughly 4 feet long and 2 feet tall. Course tan fur covered its body, with 12 to 15 black stripes marking its sloping hindquarters. The creature laired in caves by day and hunted at night. The last known thylacine died in captivity at the Hobart Zoo in 1936.

The cause of their extinction is unclear; settlers destroyed many of the animals to protect their sheep, but some scientists surmise that an epidemic wiped out the last of these creatures. The thylacine had become extinct on the mainland after the dingo was introduced. Until then it was the largest marsupial carnivore, eating roos and wallabies that it pursued until the prey was exhausted.

Tree kangaroos The early ancestors of kangaroos were mostly tree-climbers. They moved to the ground when food became more plentiful. Two species, the Lumholtz and Bennett tree kangaroos, later returned to an arboreal existence.

These two species of tree kangaroos inhabit the rainforests of northeastern Queensland. Five more species can be found in New Guinea. All have rough foot pads and curved claws for climbing. Their long, curved tails help them balance as they move from limb to limb. At times they will forage on the ground for fallen fruit and leaves.

Western gray kangaroo One of largest living marsupials, the western gray is found throughout the southern regions of Australia and on Kangaroo Island. Biologically it is similar to the eastern gray kangaroo, but it has a different reproductive cycle and darker fur. The two will not interbreed in the wild, but captive efforts have produced hybrids.

Wombat Two types of wombat inhabit the continent: the southern hairy-nosed of central South Australia, and the northern hairy-nosed of Queensland. Both live on plains and are adapted to dry habitats. As their bodies have changed to require little nitrogen, they can live on food of poor quality.

    This marsupial's closest relative is the *koala* (see), but the wombat cannot climb. Equipped to dig instead, they construct elaborate burrows that house up to three wombats. They often visit other burrows at night as they forage for grasses and roots. Although primarily nocturnal, the wombat will emerge during daylight in winter when the temperatures are cooler.

Yellow-footed marsupial mouse Known as phascogales, marsupial mice fill many niches in the Australian ecology. Roughly eight inches long, the mouse's jaws open disproportionately wide to kill and eat its insect prey. Its rigid foot pads and long claws enable it to grasp tiny cracks and crevices. The mouse can actually run upside down across the roofs of the caverns where it nests.

Yellow-footed rock wallaby This wallaby species has rough soles on its feet to more easily cling to rocks. Arching its tail over its back for balance, the rock wallaby will even climb trees with sloping trunks. They subsist on grass, herbs, leaves and fruit during times of plenty. During drought, they will eat bark and roots to obtain water.

Although they have a pouch, the mother will leave young ones in a rock crevice or other protected area while foraging in the rough terrain. This endangered species is found primarily in the Flinders Ranges of South Australia.

MONOTREMES

This is the most primitive living order of mammals, and is found nowhere else in the world. The order is small, containing only the platypus and the echidna. Both are egg-laying mammals. They possess attributes common to mammals such as fur and mammary glands, but they reproduce by laying eggs.

***

Echidna A.k.a. spiny anteater. After incubating its eggs for 10 days, the mother carries its young in a temporary abdominal pouch formed by muscular contraction. When the spines begin to develop on the babies, the mother will relax the abdominal muscles and no longer carry the young.

When threatened, the echidna will roll into a ball, wedge itself into logs, or dig a pit, leaving only a mound of bristling spines. Although it can fast for days, the echidna catches termites with a sticky tongue that can extend seven inches from its mouth.

Platypus When the first platypus skin reached Europe in the 18th century, zoologists said it was a hoax. The platypus' lineage may go back 150 million years. Mating begins in August with the courtship lasting days or even weeks. Displays include nuzzling each other's sensitive bills. They also swim in tandem as the male grasps the female's tail in his mouth. The female digs a burrow and a breeding chamber. The burrow is expanded every year, and can be 100 feet long.

The female incubates the young by holding the one to three eggs against her belly with her tail. After the eggs hatch, the female suckles the young with milk that leaks from glands on her abdomen. The male will use the hollow spur on his hind feet to compete with other males during this time; the venom gland attached to the spur does not become active until just before mating season.

Each animal will eat nearly its own weight in prawns, worms, crayfish, snails, tadpoles and insect larvae every day. The prey is located by the sensory organs on the platypus' bill, which pick up electrical impulses. The young use degenerate molars to crunch up their food; the molars are absorbed before the young are weaned, and they then grind their food between horny plates.

When not foraging, the platypus sleeps in underground tunnels with entrances just above the waterline. Due to conservation efforts, the platypus is no longer endangered.

OTHER MAMMALS

Camel The feral camels that terrorized outback settlements were single-hump Arabian camels. Today's descendants are hardier than the original breed. Camel trains were used during Australia's early history to supply remote stations and to explore new regions. They can haul 600 pounds over a long range or 1,000 pounds over a shorter distance.

In cooler weather, they can go three months without water by obtaining moisture from succulent plants. In summer, the camel can survive 10 days or more without drinking. Upon obtaining adequate water, camels will drink up to 30 gallons in ten minutes. Contrary to popular belief, the animals are not strictly vegetarian and will take advantage of any food source in their harsh environment.

Feral cat Domestic cats deliberately or accidentally released to the wild have caused the extinction of at least nine species of endangered native marsupials. Parliament has proposed eliminating all cats on the Australian continent.

Dingo Unlike feral cats, the dingo is a genuine wild dog. It never barks, communicating only with whines and howls. Dingoes are thought to have arrived with the first Aboriginal people. Formerly pack animals used during kangaroo hunts, the dogs became solitary hunters and multiplied rapidly with the introduction of the rabbit.

Now the most powerful predator in Australia, dingoes mostly subsist on small marsupials, birds, and reptiles. Dingoes sport short sandy to brown fur, with the occasional black dog. Every dingo has specific white markings on various parts of its body, most notably the tip of the tail.

For a time the government conducted aerial, chemical, and bacteriological warfare in unsuccessful attempts to exterminate the dog. Although only 2% of the dingo's prey is livestock, the dingo fence was built to protect sheep. Running from the Queensland coast to the Great Australian Bight, the dingo fence covers 5,600 kilometers and is the longest fence in the world.

Pebble-mound mouse This tan rodent is found only in the hills around Tennant Creek. This 10-gram ball of fluff constructs mounds of pebbles ten yards square. Interlaced u-shaped tunnels connect the surface holes. Individual pebbles can weigh up to half the mouse's weight.

Plague rats These native rodents are rarely seen between plagues. They live in grasslands, feeding on seeds and insects, and experience population explosions during times of abundant rain.

Rabbit This rodent was introduced for sport hunting and found grassy habitat with few predators. The ensuing population explosion consumed grass meant for livestock. Germ warfare and a rabbit fence keep the population in check.

INSECTS AND ARACHNIDS

Australian cicada With a wingspread of five inches, the cicada is an impressive sight. The sound, however, is even more impressive. At full volume, a single Australian cicada can drown out a jackhammer. The parchment-like membranes between the male's abdomen and thorax vibrate to produce a hum that the female cannot hear. She detects the vibrations instead.

Bull ant These large creatures display a clever tactic for dealing with the heat. During the peak of the day's temperatures, the ants retire to their underground burrows. To help maintain steady temperatures, bull ants will drag a stick, leaf, or rock over the entrance for shade. The venom of this ant, like the venom of bees and wasps, contains histamine and can cause shock, low blood pressure, and even death.

Bushflies Believed to have descended from African bushflies, the Australian bushfly will test the patience of any human being. The flies will cling tenaciously to a human's skin, clothing, and hair. Human and cattle dung is moist enough to provide a perfect nursery for the fly's larvae. By clinging to the source, the bushflies increase their chance of laying viable eggs.

Cane beetle These voracious beetles were accidentally introduced and can decimate Queensland's sugar cane crop. Males burrow into the cane stalks and secrete a pheromone to attract passing females. Males will fight for the burrow, attempting to dislodge each other from the plant with their curved horns.

Cockroach For over 320 million years, the cockroach has skittered around the planet. Those grown in the outback are *enormous.* Think mouse-sized.

Dung beetle These critters were introduced from Africa to help disburse the tons of cattle manure. Some 2,000 species detect the smell of fresh dung and roll balls of it away to their burrows. Dung beetles also aerate the soil and decrease food source for pests.

Funnel-web spider The funnel-web's venom is one of the most toxic spider venoms worldwide. It can kill a child in an hour or an adult in days. Within minutes the victim's tongue and muscles begin to spasm, violent retching occurs, and blood pressure soars. The venom causes an overload of electrical impulses in muscles, glands, and organs. Most large animals are immune to the venom except humans and monkeys.

The spiders grow big enough to cover the lid of a soup can. They are known for their sheer ugliness. All 37 varieties live only in eastern Australia, and commonly have a brown abdomen with a black thorax and head. Fangs up to 1/3 inch long are strong enough to pierce a fingernail, and the spiders are highly aggressive. The lair is a tube of white webbing with a funnel-shaped entrance.

Green ant A.k.a. weaver ant. These lime-green critters use their own larvae as shuttlecocks. They weave their homes by touching the silk-producing larvae to the edges of live leaves held together by other ants. Aboriginal people used the ant colonies as nasal decongestants. They squeezed the nests and inhaled the aromatic compounds released by the ants.

Honey ants Certain members of the colony store sap and the sweet secretions of plants and fruits in their abdomens. The storage ants, called repletes, are fed nectar until their abdomens stretch. Hanging from the ceiling of their underground chambers, a replete that falls might be so full that it bursts. Aboriginal people dig the ants from their deep chambers as a sweet treat.

Imperial spider This spider is known as an angler because it literally fishes for insects. While hanging from a supporting thread, the spider spins another thread with a sticky droplet on the end. Swinging this in a circle, the spider entangles passing insects.

Magnetic termites These termites are sensitive to magnetic fields and build their mounds on a north-south bearing. Note that the bearing is not that of a compass, as the termites do not adjust for declination. The wedge-shaped mounds, a steely gray, maintain excellent temperature control. They are warmed by the sun in winter and cooled by their interior humidity and wall thickness in summer. Also see *termite* for general information.

Mosquito A.k.a. mozzie. Even with recent medical advancements, mosquitos are responsible for at least one million deaths every year. Spreading malaria, yellow fever, and sleeping sickness, over 3,000 species of mosquitoes inhabit regions from the tropics to the Arctic. Mozzies find their prey by detecting carbon monoxide and warmth.

Redback spider No one in Australia has been killed by the redback since 1956 when antitoxin was developed. The redback wields a neurotoxic venom that causes profuse sweating, restricted breathing, convulsions, intense pain, temporary paralysis, and death. The redback prefers dark, cluttered areas such as those found in suburban backyards, and is infamous for hiding beneath the seats of outdoor toilets.

Indonesia and India also have redbacks, and the North American black widow spider is believed to be a close cousin. After September 11, 1996 when the first redback invaders were found in Japan, the country took drastic measures to rid itself of the pest.

Termites Termites are considered to be the oldest form of organized civilization. Over the course of 10 years, a single queen will lay 20 to 30 thousand eggs each day. There might be as many termites in a single mound as there are people in a large city; think thousands or even millions. With up to 800 mounds per hectare, the combined weight of termites in a given area often outweighs that of the land animals.

Foraging tunnels to spinifex hummocks provide a protected path from the nest to the food source. Termites lack the enzymes necessary to digest cellulose, or wood fiber, and do so only because of a symbiotic relationship with microorganisms in their intestines.

Although capable of making their own water metabolically, termites might transport water from deep soils during drought. Stored grass is used as a sponge to sop up moisture. The thick mound walls provide insulation and prevent water loss, and humidity can be 95% inside the mound.

Witchetty grub This grub, historically used by the Aboriginal people as a source of protein, is the larval stage of the baghouse moth caterpillar. Burrowing into the main tap root of the witchetty bush, the grub does not harm the host plant.

REPTILES

Amethystine python At 24 feet long, this is the biggest snake living in Australia. Actually an invader from New Guinea, the python has adapted well to its new home and can swallow kangaroos and wallabies weighing as much as 50 pounds.

Bearded dragon These lizards live in the northern reaches of Australia, and will puff up their bodies and inflate their beards when threatened. They may change colors from gray to brown to yellow depending on their environment.

Crocodile Two types of crocodiles are native to Australia, the *freshwater* and the *saltwater crocodiles* (see). All crocodilians are known to sing; listen at dusk and dawn for their growling roar.

Death adder One of Australia's most poisonous snakes, the death adder is also one of its most notorious. Luring prey to its hiding place with the grub-like tip of its tail, the adder is particularly prone to being stepped on. Its venom, which is 10 times more powerful than the king cobra's, kills by asphyxiation due to paralysis. The introduction of the *cane toad* (see) has lessened its numbers considerably in the northeast.

Freshwater crocodile A.k.a. Johnstone's river crocodile or freshie. The freshwater croc lives in the lagoons, billabongs and rivers of the northern coast. Its narrow, smooth snout and relatively small length of 10 feet or less sets it apart from the saltwater crocodile.

Freshies may be active during the day but wait until night to hunt birds, frogs, fish, shellfish, and small animals. Reproducing near the end of the dry season, females will lay about 20 eggs in a sandy bank. This species is not normally known to attack humans.

Goanna A.k.a. monitor lizard. The males will fight for mating rights, beginning with displays of throat swelling and loud hisses. Eventually they rear up on their hind legs and fight with teeth, claws, and a lashing tail. The goanna is one of the few creatures immune to the neurotoxins of the taipan and tiger snakes, and will gladly gobble them up. Aboriginal people often ate goannas because the meat is exceptionally tasty.

Lizard Australia is the land of lizards with up to 440 individuals per hectare. As many as 42 different species will live together in the same area, an event that has no ecological parallel anywhere else in the world. Populations may explode when termites are particularly abundant.

Perentie lizard This reptile is the second-largest monitor lizard in the world, just behind the Komodo dragon of the East Indies. Despite its size, it is shy and non-aggressive unless cornered. Usually found in the northern or central regions, they are more scarce than the goanna.

Saltwater crocodile A.k.a. estuarine crocodile or saltie. This leviathan can grow up to 25 feet long and has been known to deliberately hunt humans. Salties live in rivers and swamps, occasionally in freshwater lagoons or the sea. Their diet consists mainly of crustaceans, fish, reptiles, birds and small mammals, but salties won't hesitate to take advantage of any food source.

Hiding inches under murky water, saltwater crocodiles can stay submerged for 2 ½ hours waiting for prey to drink. They can catch birds in flight and have been known to knock bats from the air with their tails. Protected since 1979, the population has increased to the point where the crocs are a very real threat to unwary humans.

Snake Australia harbors 11 of the deadliest snakes in the world. Just saying.

Thorny devil A.k.a. horned dragon or mountain devil. This shy, seven-inch lizard is covered with sharp spines sprouting from conical mounds on its body, including horn-like spikes over each eye. Found in the deserts of central Australia and other dry regions, the lizard is active by day and disappears in burrows or under shrubs at night.

The brown and tan patterns on its skin are excellent camouflage in the desert. The thorny devil can change color, turning darker in cool weather to absorb the sun's energy and brighter in warm weather to reflect heat. The lizard also channels dew to its mouth through grooves on its skin.

White salt dragon This tiny monitor lizard, inhabiting the 4,000 square miles of the Lake Eyre salt pan, eats one of the few other living creatures in the area: ants. Its sunken eyes are shielded from the glare by serrated eyelids, and its nostrils are slits to help filter out the blowing salt.

Water snake See entry for *sea snake* under Marine Life.

AMPHIBIANS

Cane toads A.k.a. marine toads. This species was introduced from South America to eat the *cane beetles* (see), but developed a taste for local marsupials, other toads, frogs and lizards. Cane toads can weight six pounds and can grow large enough to cover a dinner plate. Poison in glands located behind the toad's eyes swiftly kills any would-be predators.

Surprisingly, the toads are often kept as pets for children. The creatures are phlegmatic enough not to secrete any poisons without very rough handling. In small doses, the poison is a hallucinogenic, so the dried skins have been rolled into illegal cigarettes.

Corroboree toad Another creature which has made incredible adaptations is Australia's corroboree toad. Living high in the cold mountains, it lays about a dozen eggs on damp sphagnum moss or under snow, the few sources of moisture. At the next rain or thaw, the eggs are washed into puddles and begin their development. If rains or the thaw are delayed too long, the tadpoles will begin to develop inside the eggs.

Tree frog The giant tree frog can grow up to six inches across. Its large webbed feet allow it to climb trees. The frog prefers to live on the ground and usually climbs only to forage for food. They can squeeze into small spaces, and can compress their bodies enough to hide beneath tree bark.

MARINE LIFE

Anemone Related to corals and jellyfish, this creature is basically a tube anchored to the sea floor. The open end of the tube, the anemone's mouth, is ringed by tentacles that catch prey. In some species, the tentacles shoot barbs packing a sting similar to that of a coral. Other anemones catch their prey with sticky threads. Some use fighting tentacles to attack their neighbors. Those with sweeper tentacles can reach 10 times further than other anemones.

When human skin touches the tentacles, itching or swelling results. Anemones can be eaten cooked, but an uncooked member of a particular species was once a method of suicide in Samoa.

Australian sea lion These sea lions, one of the rarest seal species in the world, live on islands off the southern and western coasts. High concentrations of the creatures occur at Seal Bay on Kangaroo Island and at Dangerous Reef off Port Lincoln. Although nearly wiped out due to the early fur trade, the sea lions are now protected by law.

The highly aggressive males will protect females and young, but have been known to savage sleeping pups. Females will protect the pups of other females who are off feeding. At age two, males become larger and bulkier in preparation for mating battles, and their fur becomes darker brown.

Blue-ringed octopus The blue-ringed octopus is about five inches long and packs a venomous bite that can kill a human. When disturbed, its markings turn electric blue to warn off predators. See *octopus* for general information.

Chambered nautilus The nautilus is a chambered cephalopod known for its unusual shell, a buoyant white home with tan stripes. As the creature grows, it builds a larger chamber outside its current one. When the chamber is complete, the creature moves in and then seals off the old chamber with mother-of-pearl. The siphuncle, a tiny organ running through all the chambers, removes the fluid in the old chamber and replaces it with nitrogen.

Clownfish A.k.a. anemone fish. Pairs of this colorful four-inch fish live in a symbiotic relationship with sea anemones. The fish exude a mucous coating similar to the anemone's, and are protected from predators by the anemone's sting. The clownfish clean the anemone by eating scraps of food and debris that lodge between its tentacles. The clownfish may also act as a lure to attract other fish. When the larger female dies, the male changes sex and takes another male as a partner.

Cone shell These gastropods are about two to four inches long with beautifully patterned shells. They harpoon prey with a hollow barb, inject venom, and reel in the victim. The creature may expel itself from the shell to envelope or swallow its prey, during which time it is vulnerable. The cone shell's venom is so toxic that 27 people have died from its sting.

Coral These animals, members of the polyp species, are literally the size of pinheads. Corals are classified as hard or soft depending on whether they secrete calcium carbonate to create an outer skeleton. Soft corals have internal skeletons of sclerites, tiny crystalline structures.

The corals of the *Great Barrier Reef* (see) will grow only in temperatures from 65 to 96° F. While the reef can be a thousand feet deep in some parts, corals only grow near the surface where they can obtain sunlight. Corals live in a symbiotic relationship with an algae that requires sunlight to photosynthesize. The algae's waste products provide the nutrients the polyps need to produce calcium carbonate.

Crown-of-thorns starfish This starfish eats coral, and during population explosions, it wipes out communities on the *Great Barrier Reef* (see). Government-paid divers pluck as many as 50,000 crown-of-thorns starfish a season to protect the reef.

Dolphin These playful creatures mate belly to belly, just as humans do. They engage in a form of sonic foreplay, culminating in a brief spat of intercourse during which the male swims beneath the female. Each dolphin has a name, a signature whistle that other dolphins in the pod recognize. They sleep, with one eye open to danger, for about an hour every evening.

Giant clam The giant clam grows to more than two feet in diameter. At that size, it is strong enough to trap a diver. The mantle, the fleshy portion that is exposed, comes in blue, purple, and green hues.

Great Barrier Reef This is the world's largest coral creation at 1,250 miles long. Covering a total area of 80,000 square miles, the Great Barrier Reef can be seen from space. Lying between 10 and 200 miles off shore, the reef has been growing for nearly 8,000 years. Near shore, lagoons and pools up to 200 feet deep showcase coral and plants when the tides recede.

In November, sea temperatures rise. A few days after the full moon, millions of coral egg and sperm packets engulf the reef. Every coral on the reef spawns within hours of each other to create the most spectacular breeding display in nature.

Great white shark A.k.a. white death. The great whites are found mostly along the southern coast where they feed on seals. Although food is abundant, the white death attacks more humans than any other shark species. At an average of 26 feet long, the shark can swallow an adult whole and has been known to attack boats until they sink. Also see general information under the entry for *shark*.

Humpback whale One of the baleen whales, humpbacks feed by straining water through the plates in their upper jaws. Humpbacks will herd krill with a trail of bubbles released beneath the school, and then lunge through the center with their mouth open.

This species makes its annual migration run up the Western Coast of Australia and back. After spending six months in the cold Arctic waters, they head north to winter in the tropics. Humpbacks can be seen July through October from Heron Island to the Whitsunday Islands.

AMAZING AUSTRALIA

Compared to other species, the humpback's blow is wide for its height, and its flippers are enormous. Females typically calve once every two to three years. The song sung during mating is sung by all males. During the course of the season, the song is gradually changed. At the end of the season the song will be entirely different, but it will be sung by every male in the group.

Mudskipper Occasionally bodies of water dry up, leaving the inhabitants to die a gruesome death. The mudskipper, however, has pectoral fins specially adapted to move over land. Tough fin rays and muscles link the fins to the skeleton. The fish pulls itself forward with the fins. It can also anchor its tail in the mud and flip itself through the air.

Nudibranch A.k.a. sea slug. These mollusks have lost their shells and are defended with bright coloration, strong odors, and a foul taste. The aeolid ingests the toxins from the stinging cells of the coral it eats. The poison collects in the feathery protrusions along its back and discourages predators.

Octopus The octopus is a cephalopod without a shell. The largest octopus on record boasted a tentacle span of 32 feet, but most are only 1 to 2 feet across. If severed, the tentacles can regenerate, but procreation proves deadly to the female. After building a shelter for her 50,000 or so eggs, she guards the structure for six months without eating and eventually dies.

Most species can change color to reflect mood, to warn off predators or invaders, or for camouflage. Pigmented cells suffuse color throughout the skin in seconds. Color changes made to indicate sexual availability are ruled by hormones instead of the nervous system, and usually take longer to appear.

Parrot fish The teeth of the parrot fish have fused into a hard protrusion used to scrape algae from coral. During periods of rest, it secretes a mucous coating for protection.

Portuguese man-of-war This jellyfish floats like a blue ball and dangles tentacles as much as 20 meters below the surface. The tentacles sting small fish to death. To drag the meal up to the polyp's mouth, the tentacles contract to as little as half an inch long. The man-of-war relies solely on the wind to propel it through the ocean.

Queensland lungfish This creature is a living fossil, a primitive marine species that thrived during the Triassic period 35 million years ago. The lungfish can live out of water in dry mud for the summer months. While it normally breaths through gills and surfaces every few minutes to breath air into its single lung, the fish will drown if held underwater for too long.

Sea snakes Sea snakes are small and shy, but can be deadly if they bite a human in defense. Most live in the outer reef areas where fewer humans visit. Each species relies to a varying degree on skin breathing, and absorbs oxygen directly from the air. Some species release nitrogen through their skin to prevent the bends during their deep dives.

Sea turtle Loggerhead and green turtles are common visitors to the shallow waters of the Great Barrier Reef. They nest on coral cays and occasionally on the mainland. Sea turtles have flippers instead of toes like their land turtle cousins. They also cannot fully retract their heads into their shells. Males spend their entire lives at sea, while females return to the beach where they were born to lay eggs.

A female can live decades before she is ready to lay, at which time she will come ashore every two to three years. Nesting occurs several times during those years. Eggs are laid during high tide on the highest point of beach, and the young are born during another high tide when the water is close. Adults swim thousands of miles before migrating back to nesting beaches.

Shark About one-third of all shark species lay eggs. The rest give birth to live young. Embryos will occasionally cannibalize their siblings in utero, and the female sand tiger releases hundreds of eggs during gestation to feed her two embryos. Sharks can detect the electric impulses of animals buried beneath the sand.

Sponge These primitive, single-celled animals have colonized every sea at every depth. A few are even found in fresh water. The sponges include almost 10,000 species, some of which have remained unchanged for 500 million years. They occur in a variety of sizes, from less than an inch to over 100 pounds.

They can be shaped like fans, domes, balls, or cups. Colors range through brown and deep red into white, and the skeletal structure is similar to chalk, crystal or rawhide. Although they have no organs, nerves or muscles, sponges sift food particles from the water and help keep the ocean clean. These creatures make up the largest group of animals on the *Great Barrier Reef* (see).

Stonefish A relative of the Scorpaenidae family, the stonefish is well camouflaged as it lies motionless on the bottom waiting for its next meal. Unfortunately, this makes it prone to being stepped on. The 13 poisonous dorsal spines transfer venom to the wound, causing severe pain, swelling, and even death.

BIRDS

Australian king parrot This bird is identified by its cap of orange feathers. It lives on the coastal regions of eastern Australia, and eats seeds, nuts, and fruit.

Australian pelican The Australian pelican's piebald body grows up to 5 feet long. The wingspan can be 7 feet. The long bill and deep pouch are used to capture fish, and the bird prefers water no deeper than the length of its bill and neck. Flocks are cooperative fishers. They swish their bills through the water to drive fish into the shallows. The pelicans will usually be found on calm waters as they need a smooth surface from which to take off.

Black swan Coal black except for its red beak and legs, and its white wing tips, the black swan is Western Australia's elegant state bird. After building floating nests of reeds in marshlands, black swan pairs will raise eight or nine chicks. Pairs will often gather into flocks to live on rivers and lakes.

Booby Three distinct species of boobies may inhabit the same coral cays on the Barrier Reef. The red-footed booby nests among trees and shrubs, the brown booby prefers cliffs or clearings near bushes, and the masked booby makes its home in large clearings.

Bower bird The male bower bird creates some of the most elaborate structures in the animal kingdom for its courtship ritual. The structures can take months to build and can include tunnels, walls, fences, or borders. The structures are decorated with butterfly wings, iridescent beetle carapaces, flowers, and other shiny or colorful objects, depending on the species.

Brolga A.k.a. Australian crane. These steel-blue cranes are four feet tall and have red heads. Subsisting on plant tubers, seeds, insects and maize during the dry, the birds live in the northern and eastern regions of the continent. Their nests are low platforms of grass built on a high place in a swamp.

Their courtship rituals, performed in groups of hundreds on plains and in swamps, include dancing, leaping, high steps, and fluttering and arching of their wings. While tossing their heads, they might throw sticks into the air. Pairs join together in exuberant calls. The dance of the brolga forms the basis of many corroborees and has inspired modern ballet.

Cassowary Similar in appearance to the emu, the cassowary is also flightless. The bird stands about four feet tall with colorful markings on its bald head and neck. A horny protrusion called a casque protects the bird's skull as it plunges head-first through the thick tropical jungles. The bird eats fallen fruit, fungi, snails, and carrion.

AMAZING AUSTRALIA

Cassowaries are solitary except during breeding season. The female visits just long enough to mate and lay the eggs that the male will incubate. The bird makes a rumbling noise when it encounters something new. If threatened, the bird will hiss and raise its feathers. The sharp outer talons on each foot make for a formidable defense, and cassowaries have disemboweled careless tourists.

Corella These birds are cockatoos with small crests and white bodies. Somehow the corella ends up looking like a wizened old aunt, but is just as playful as the *sulphur-crested cockatoo* (see). They are able to find abundant seeds during the dry, and so tend to clown around quite often to fill their days.

Crested tern This seabird nests on the coral cays of the Great Barrier Reef. Each nest will be precisely placed in relation to its neighbors, close enough to conserve space and afford group protection, but just out of pecking distance. As amazing as it sounds, every bird sitting on a nest in a rookery will face the same direction.

Emu This bird is featured on the national coat of arms. About five feet tall and 120 pounds, the flightless bird can run over 30 mph and deliver a powerful kick. They prefer to travel in flocks and are nomadic. Like other birds, emus will swallow pebbles and charcoal to help its gizzard grind the seeds, fruit, leaves, flowers, and insects it eats.

The male takes sole responsibility for incubating the five to eleven eggs and caring for the young. During incubation, the male does not eat, drink, or defecate. The female usually leaves to mate with other males, but might occasionally stay to watch the chicks hatch.

Fairy penguin A.k.a. little penguin or southern blue penguin. Found on the coast of southern Australia and on offshore islands, the fairy penguin swims out to sea every day to fish. It wades ashore at night to escape predators. Swimming at speeds up to 1,000 feet per minute, the penguin is ungainly on land. To escape predators, it might slide on its belly down sand dunes into the water.

Rookeries consist of hundreds of individuals, although an occasional pair may isolate themselves in a rock crevice or under a shrub. The typical nest is a burrow about four feet long lined with sticks, seaweed, and grass.

Kookaburra The kookaburra is best known for its call, a chuckle that builds to maniacal laughter. This kingfisher has forgotten how to fish, and eats rats, mice, and snakes instead. The bird may drop snakes from a great height or crack the creature against a tree or rock to kill it. The kookaburra will also dive into shallow water to capture prey or to bathe.

The birds can live over 20 years, during which a pair will bond and stay together to raise their young. The young will stay with the parents for three to four years, helping to raise other young and to defend territory.

Lyrebird Just under four feet long, this bird sports magnificent plumage during the breeding season. As beautiful as the lacy feathers are, though, the bird is best known for its voice. Its bubbling songs are sung alongside those of other birds, as the lyrebird will copy the calls of its neighbors.

The shimmying dance it performs during courtship, the spread of delicate, silvery plumage, and its voice combine to woo even the shyest female. After the breeding season, the male loses its showy feathers and blends into the forest once again.

Mallee fowl This native pheasant is found in mallee scrubland where it roosts in the shade by day. On a diet of seeds, fruit, and insects, the bird will spend 11 months a year involved in breeding activities. Early in the year, a pair will dig a pit and line it with forest debris. Over months the pile grows, some reaching 20 feet in diameter and 3 feet in height.

The temperature is checked throughout the day, and debris is removed or added to maintain a constant temperature of 100°F. Over three weeks, the female lays 16 to 33 eggs 18 inches below the surface. Eventually the mound is abandoned as the temperature becomes too difficult to maintain, and the chicks hatch and dig themselves out without assistance.

Mopoke A.k.a. tawny wide-mouth. This bird is a member of the nightjar family, and is characterized by its wide, hooked beak and mottled plumage. By compressing its feathers and pointing its head, the bird camouflages itself as a branch or old stump. When threatened, it leans forward and opens its beak and large yellow eyes wide.

The mopoke is widespread in forested areas and some suburbs throughout Australia, subsisting on a diet of insects, lizards, and small animals. It doesn't hesitate to feed on carrion, and road kills of this bird are common.

Osprey This seabird lands feet first in the water, and may submerge completely to catch its prey. It enjoys a 90% capture rate, the highest of any raptor. The feathers are compact to cut down on air resistance during dives, and rough padding on the feet helps the bird grip prey.

During courtship, the osprey will perform aerial displays. A pair will build a huge nest that they will maintain for years. There is only one type of osprey, but it is the most widely distributed species in the world.

Paradise parrot Most parrots live in trees, but this parrot hollows out termite mounds for its nesting chamber. Even the nest itself is lined with the papery debris of the tunnels. The termites finish off the chamber for the birds by sealing everything with clay to preserve the humidity inside the mound.

Rainbow lorikeet This is the most colorful of all lorikeet species. Groups up to several hundred strong can be seen drinking from sprinklers or roosting in trees throughout Australia. Like other lorikeets, the rainbow lorikeet subsists mostly on nectar that it laps up with the tip of its brush-like tongue.

Raven Ravens and crows, their smaller cousins, are ubiquitous throughout Australia. Ravens are highly intelligent birds with astounding memories. Their adaptability means that even in the face of development, ravens are expanding their territories. Their wing span averages four feet.

AMAZING AUSTRALIA

Scrub turkey One of two incubator birds in Australia, the scrub turkey builds mounds of forest debris as large as 35 feet in diameter and 15 feet high. The rotting vegetation provides heat and the eggs are laid inside.

The male uses his beak to test the temperature, and sand and other debris are piled on top to preserve warmth. During the heat of the afternoon, the male will scratch away layers to maintain a consistent temperature. As the cool night approaches, he adds them back. See also *mallee fowl*.

Shearwater These seabirds are ungainly on land due to their webbed feet, and usually nest on a cliff. When they wish to fly, they use a low-energy approach and simply fall off the cliff.

Spinifex pigeon This outback denizen eats plant seeds and spinifex flowers; with its low metabolic rate, it needs little food. To further conserve energy, the pigeons will roost together at night to share heat. They walk nearly everywhere except when searching for water. In breeding season, the male bows as a threat gesture to other males and will attack with its wings.

Spoonbill The edge of the spoonbill's beak is so sensitive it can detect prey by touch as the bird sweeps its bill through the water. During mating displays, the birds will nuzzle each other's bills. As the birds eat foods rich in carotene, their feathers take on a pale coloration.

Sulphur-crested cockatoo Widespread throughout Australia wherever trees grow, the sulphur-crested cockatoo is perhaps the noisiest and most rambunctious of birds. While the flock feeds on seeds, berries, insects and larvae, several sentries stand guard.

Tasmanian native hen A.k.a. narkie or waterhen. This small bird is rather aggressive, and will loudly and exuberantly defend its territory. It will swim or run to escape danger, but rarely flies unless pressed.

The native hen lives alone or in small groups near water or in swamps. During breeding season, hens build nests in a shallow depression lined with grass, roots, leaves, or twigs. Hidden in the undergrowth, hens will deposit up to nine brown-speckled eggs.

Wedge-tailed eagle This eagle is the largest bird of prey in Australia, and has a wingspan of over eight feet. Although it feeds mainly on rabbits, lizards, birds and small animals, it is not adept at capturing live prey and relies heavily on carrion. This habit leads to many road kills as they scavenge from the highways.

Willy wagtail This piebald rogue has a call that sounds like BB pellets dropping onto a sheet of metal. The flipping of its tail, for which it is famous, helps flush insects from the surrounding dust and scrub.

The Dance

An Australian Aboriginal Dreamtime Guide to Living with Passion

Adapted from *Seven Sisters:*

Spiritual Messages from Aboriginal Australia

Back in the Dreamtime, a stunning young woman loved to dance. She whirled and twirled for the sheer joy of movement, for the bliss of feeling the wind whisper across her skin. Men and women from every tribe stared. Even the spirits that lived in the sky and the earth and the air watched her.

Despite the endless suitors who visited, she took neither a lover nor a husband. The chores of a wife and mother would leave little time for practice. Many people pressured her to marry because they didn't think she would dedicate her entire life to her art. They couldn't imagine making that kind of sacrifice themselves, so they were unable to imagine it in anyone else.

One man agreed with the naysayers. He was a bachelor and tried endlessly to woo the dancer. When she would not make a place in her life for him, he decided to steal her away and force her to become his wife. She could still dance…after she gave birth to the babies and gathered the family's food and captured small game for their daily meals and cooked the meat of the large animals he killed. Then she could dance as much as she liked.

When the wind spirits brushed against the bachelor, they discovered his plan. The spirits rushed across the desert to find the dancer. They painted her skin with invisible ochre and whispered magic words. Throwing back her head, she shut her eyes and spun into a trancelike dance. She did not see how her body was changing; she felt only the ecstasy of becoming.

The bachelor arrived and lunged for his prize. Just then, the magic whispers fell silent. The dancer's arms had become wings and the wind lifted her beyond his reach. She had become the brolga, a steel-blue crane that dances its joyful courtship in Australia's northern marshland.

True transcendence occurs when passion and creativity lead you to your divine self. No suitor or elder or friend can force you to become that which you are not meant to be. Only you can decide to dance on the winds that support you, only you can connect with the spirits and energies that will shape-shift you into new life.

In this story, a young woman was promised the best marriage and a dedicated husband. But that vision of perfection belonged to people who believed that a satisfying life looked like everyone else's. The mainstream version of happiness would have suppressed the dancer's true joy.

People are as individual as river rocks. Not everyone will be happy in the deepest current, the lifestyle defined as normal. If you are one of those unique individuals, you must dedicate yourself to achieving what is best for you. What you sacrifice won't matter. Passion will point the way to the contribution only you can make. Passion will bring you back to yourself...and guide you to your true joy.

Even when others disbelieve, even when they talk about you and to you as if your passion could easily be turned to other pursuits, you must hold true to yourself. When people try to saddle you with their own limits, thank them for speaking their truth and recognize that those limits are not your own.

Along the way, avoid the shadows that threatened the dancer. Since no one was courageous or outrageous enough to be her friend or true lover, she was dangerously isolated. Her passion became a dark undertow. Left in human form, she would have danced herself to death.

The bachelor had already been swept away by his own rip current. He adored the young woman yet he did not really love her. No one did. They could not truly love her because they did not believe that her passion was real. If they had, their love would have transcended mainstream expectations.

From cradle to grave, we must recognize that expectations are nothing more than guidelines. They can create pathways for people who are floundering but should never become prisons. Individuals who veer off are our entrepreneurs and our geniuses, our small business owners and our Einsteins. When individuals follow their dreams, they benefit everyone.

This is the message sent to us from the Dreamtime. When we pursue our passion, when we generate our own bliss, we spread our joy to everyone around us. Dance your dream into life and you dance for us all.

LAINE CUNNINGHAM

AMAZING AUSTRALIA

For more Aboriginal stories paired with advice
on happiness and success, grab
Seven Sisters
Spiritual Messages from Aboriginal Australia.

To take a trip through the Outback, read
Woman Alone
A Six-Month Journey Through the Australian Outback.

Kids will enjoy
How Kangaroo Got Its Tail
Australian Aboriginal Stories for Young Readers.

Also by Laine Cunningham

Novels
The Family Made of Dust
Beloved
Reparation

Travel Books
Woman Alone
A Six-Month Journey Through the Australian Outback

On the Wallaby Track
Essential Australian Words and Phrases

Seven Sisters
Spiritual Messages from Aboriginal Australia

The Travel Photo Art Series
Bikes of Berlin
Necropolises of New Orleans I & II
Ruins of Rome I & II
Ancients of Assisi I & II
Panoramas of Portugal
Nuances of New York
Impressions of Italy
Utopia of the Unicorn

Other Nonfiction

The Zen for Life Series
The Zen of Travel
The Zen of Gardening
Zen in the Stable
The Zen of Chocolate
The Zen of Dogs

The Wisdom for Life Series
The Wisdom of Puppies
The Wisdom of Babies
The Wisdom of Weddings

Writing While Female or Black or Gay
Diverse Voices in Publishing

How Kangaroo Got Its Tail
Australian Aboriginal Stories for Young Readers

www.ingramcontent.com/pod-product-compliance
Lightning Source LLC
Chambersburg PA
CBHW070035040426
42333CB00040B/1678